nine lives

katherine may

BookLeaf
Publishing

India | USA | UK

Presentation by *BookLeaf Publishing*

Web: www.bookleafpub.com

E-mail: info@bookleafpub.com

ISBN: 9789357446563

First edition 2022

DEDICATION

for h; because i'm just glad you exist.

ACKNOWLEDGE MENT

with many thanks to raw sakura press for their micro-residency.
this is a version of the work that was produced.
to keep for a version of myself.

PREFACE

have the platter ready,
i'll bring the cheese knife.

PREFACE

have the platter ready,
i'll bring the cheese knife.

1.

i want to write about being kissed
i want to write about watching my body change,
       small to big and then small again
i want to write about my hands in the grass
i want to write about hearing you laugh for the
first time,
       crinkling your eyes and smiling
i want to write about people in the old days
i want to write about my family learning their
language,
       consonants and intonations
i want to dream about being kissed!
i want to dream about not watching anything at
all!
i want to dream about your hands around a
branch!
i want to dream about those people loving!
i want to dream about about my ancestors being
proud of me!!

2.

there is an ugliness in a healthy love.
a monstrosity in not aching for
someone/something
>not feeling that one touch could kill you.

there is a strangeness in a healthy mind.
a monstrosity in not yearning for
something/someone
>not hoping that one thought would kill
you.

3.

there is an ugliness in a healthy love.
a monstrosity in not aching for
someone/something
      not feeling that one touch could kill you.

there is a strangeness in a healthy mind.
a monstrosity in not yearning for
something/someone
      not hoping that one thought would kill
you.

4.

"I am a wound walking out of hospital.
I am a wound that they are letting go."

the word hospital has eight letters
eight times have i been admitted to a hospital

first i was born,
second i reacted.

every time i go and they check me
they check me for things they can't seem to see

third i heard a ringing,
(and a reprieve was in years)
fourth my body ached.

i hold my mum's hand as she talks
she talks as i sit there legs under blanket

fifth my mind broke,
(and a stay was for weeks)
sixth i swallowed too much.

the word hospital has eight letters
eight times i have been admitted to a hospital

seven and eight were the same,
eight and seven i reacted again.

"I am a wound walking out of hospital.
I am a wound that they are letting go."

5.

i dont want to keep thinking this or that or them
or they i dont want to miss out on something or
anything or nothing theres nothing i dont want to
edit or write or read or remember i dont want a
memory of him or her or together over there i
want to feel detached and mismatched and feel
ready to be dispatched but they lost my package
in the mail unable to locate and i want to stay
unable to locate i want to throw away my phone
and my brain and the thoughts all inside and the
people who decide that we're here but we're not
and i want to still feel you and take you with me
and feel you always beside me inside me reside
with me always in the motel and the lodge and
the house across the street i dont want to move
or be still or lay down or sit up straight i dont
want to keep thinking that im done im done im
done but im here im here im here can you hear
can you hear can you hear the way they whisper
when i close my eyes i squeeze them shut and
feel dizzy and nice and i eat berries and rice and
cook noodles and bake and find bread and sticks
and light a fire and burn my hands and rip at the
skin and peel it all back and the fruit drips and
you kiss me and i kiss you back and i dont want
to forget any of that. ill remember just a little bit
of that.

6.

i don't like the way he's making me think!!
i don't love him like that but why can't he!!
i don't like the feeling that he's using me!!
i don't love that he has no way of being safe!!

i don't like cherry ripe ice cream!!
i don't love that it's all i taste of him!!
i don't like like that i obsess over these things!!
   i don't love it.
      i don't want it,
anymore.

01.

i want to rip my skin off. lay it down neatly and fold into thirds; then thirds again. i will wash it slowly in the bathtub. full of bubbles and soap, i will clean it of all my thoughts of you. i will scrub evenly the scars you left behind; exfoliate the false love you gave.

i want to rip my skin off. cut it up into a million tiny pieces with craft scissors. the ones that zig-zag through paper and make a child laugh. i will throw each piece in a paper bag. go out to the woods and bury them each a metre apart. i will bury with them all my thoughts of you. i will soil the sores you burned in me; beat out the promises you made.

i want to rip my skin off. rough and full of pain, screaming you out of me as my hands bloody and cripple. i will let the saltiness of my crying burn my cheeks. seeping into raw muscle and nerve, i will sit on the cold bathroom floor; make my own stains in the grout where you stood thinking of me. i will never grow back what you took from me.

02.

i love it when men are women and women are
men.
i love it when one becomes another and another
becomes one.

i love it when he holds his hand out for me to
take.
i love it when my fingers curl nearly into his.

i love it how i feel everything and nothing all at
once.
i love it how he tells me something that can
mean anything.

i love it how in the dark i'm the man and you're
my woman.
i love it how we become each other when it's
cold outside.

03.

when i was 5 i wrote a song
when i was 6 i sang it for my dad
when i was 7 i learnt it on guitar
when i was 8 i entered the talent show
when i was 9 my friends joined in
when i was 10 i broke my hand
when i was 11 i lost my guitar
when i was 12 i got my tonsils out
when i was 13 i auditioned for the choir
when i was 14 i wrote a different song
when i was 15 i sang it for myself
when i was 16 i wrote it down and gave it away
when i was 17 i had it sung back to me
when i was 18 i heard they crashed their car
when i was 19 i cried hearing one note of it
when i was 20 i did nothing.
        i was 20 and they weren't there.
        i was 20 and they were still a teen.
        i was 20 and every song hurt to hear.
        i was 20 and i shuddered at the sound of
strings.
when i turned 21 i tried the piano.
when i turned 22 i covered lily allen.
when i turned 23 i joined a band.
when i turned 24 my life became the car crash.

i was 24 and they weren't there.
i was 24 and they were still a teen.
i was 24 and kicked out of the band.
i was 24 and kicked out of my own

head.

i stayed 24 like they stayed 18.
6 years of distance between us.
they welcomed me with open

arms;

singing my song.
softly asking what took me so long.

04.

he says that "man is the only being who knows he is alone, and the only one who seeks out another." is that true? am i but a man feeling his lonesome? am i not a woman who feels a different kind of solitude? am i but a woman at all? i only feel woman enough when someone, a man, is inside me. i only feel woman enough when i'm able to let him. even if it's forced it's i who's forced it. am i not allowed to be a man all alone? what is a man when he is all alone? away even from himself. where does he sit? does he lie down and weep? where is he in regard to this woman? where is he in regard to me? there is often talk of a horrified existence. a weakness in the terror; in the terror of knowing one's shadow. our only shadow. do we dance along the shapes against the wall? do we hide when it's not looking? is there enough horror in knowing that the shadow is only ever us? is that what it means to be alone? to know we are connected to something else but to nothing else at all. and when the man is inside something else. someone else. are the shadows dancing? or are they dying?

05.

i am nine pages in to the book you gave me
      i am nine lives in to the love we share

i am nine songs in to the rhythm of your heart
      i am nine reasons in to not letting you go

i am nine seats in to the movie theatre we met
      i am nine metres in to the bath water

i am nine drinks in to the night you confessed to
me
      i am nine hours in to racking up the
courage

i am nine buses in to the long road home
      i am nine episodes in to our favourite
show

i am nine petals in to those roses i still keep
      i am nine globes in to your shining light

i am nine pills in to driving myself crazy
      i am nine hairs in to pulling out my
scalp

i am nine hours in to saying goodbye for the first
time
        i am nine days late.

i am nine months in to this thing you forgot
about
        she is nine years in to not knowing you.

06.

moonlight
in a quiet garden
that is her beauty

that is where she lays her head
that is the place of angels
that is a sight only for us

moonlight
in a quiet garden
that is her beauty

in a sweet old memory
in a delicate romance
in a surrender where we forget

moonlight
in a quiet garden
that is her beauty

moonlight! my darling
moonlight!! it's only true
moonlight!!! out here in the open

001.

it is only in me that i find you
      a little being that didn't get to be
not in the way you wanted to
      you'd always laugh and call me names
like 'morning wood'
           and 'my number two soulmate'

i remember our matching green jackets
      big and fluffy round the collar
in the yard smoking something
      on the train showing me something
like a stupid meme
         or an old photo with your head
shaved

it's in strange memories i hear you
      a very short friendship we had
but it was fast and immersive
      the way you'd tower over me
like some kind of older brother
        younger than me still growing

another party place you'd be going
      running into each other with fast food
meeting at the steps of the library

in your work uniform and singing songs
like an old justin bieber
                or a classic michael jackson

the last time i saw you was in laughter
        one more nickname as i said a quick bye
you sat at the desk getting high
        giggling and smiling and a child
like nothing was wrong
                and things weren't hard to get
through

months went by when i heard
        a friend casually saying it in a text
'oh by the way' as if you hadn't been hurting
        but it was such a dark thing to say
like losing an extra limb
                like a guardian you only noticed
once gone

so many years later i still think of it
        the flippancy of such a friend
how she didn't think we mattered together
        were close in any sense of the word
like cousins who didn't know
                like the two of us even mattered
at all…

002.

why does it hurt to love someone like that
          why doesn't it hurt to love someone like
that

why will it be hard to say goodbye to you
          why won't it be hard to say goodbye to
you

why can things change in such an instance
          why can't things change in such an
instance

why does nothing feel the right kind of way
          why doesn't anything feel the right kind
of way

                    i look for you in all the dark
places
                    i see you in all the streets
different faces
                    i hope you're okay but i hope
that you're not
                    i leave every door unlocked
letting out the rot

why doesn't anything feel the right kind of way
        why does nothing feel the right kind of
way

why can't things change in such an instance
        why can things change in such an
instance

why won't it be hard to say goodbye to you
        why will it be hard to say goodbye to
you

why doesn't it hurt to love someone like that
        why does it hurt to love someone like
that

003.

angel number 222

                    everything
          will turn out
      for the best.

004.

here i pour us each a glass of milk
here i place it upon the table
here i listen to you gulp
here i hear you ask for more
here i push over mine still full
here i see you sip it in shame
here i sit and watch you still
here i open my eyes even more
here i reach for the near empty carton

(here i pour you two glasses of milk.)

005.

everyone i've ever loved leaves in the morning.
they don't bother saying anything true.
it's like i'm not worth an ounce of that decency.
and when i try to speak my throat splinters.
i just want to be loved the way i love them.
being wanted is an aphrodisiac of the highest
degree.
i'm not sure what it's like to feel calm and
content.
i keep thinking that today with be the real thing.
there's only so much one person can choose to
take.
i am a saint and a sinner and need to rehearse.
only in doing a practice run do i feel safe.
i owe people so much but they owe me just the
same.
i write silly little lines and smoke long gusts of
wind.
the being inside me eats away at my liver.
i take big strong swigs of gasoline to rest.
it's christmas and easter and our own
thanksgiving.
i feel pregnant and empty and a phantom in my
hands.

don't ask me what things mean i'm just here to
look.
it's one hundred years into the future that i can
smell.
the pain between my eyes is from those same
years ago.
i wear an old dress and pray to the old gods.
there comes the new ghosts to take me away.
again everyone i love leaves me in the morning.

006.

"Then it comes to me:
Yes I'll die, so will everyone, so has everyone.
It's what we have in common.
And for a moment, the sorrow ceased, and I saw
that it hadn't been sorrow after all, but
loneliness,"

A loneliness that haunts me
every October. A loneliness that Libra season
gives me every year. A loneliness that only my
grandmother could come back and cure. A
loneliness that only my father knows how to fill.
A loneliness that my best friend enters me with.
A loneliness that my cat escaped from.

Marie Howe, from Magdalene: Poems;
"October"

0001.

I only know who I am when I see you.

I only know where I place when I'm with you.

I only know I'm alive when I touch you.

I only know anything because of you!

"I barely knew I had skin until I met you."

I only know secrets because of you!

I only know heart because of you!

I only know emotion because of you!

"I barely knew I had skin until I met you."

Sarah Waters, from The Paying Guests

0002.

"I was very young when I was cracked open.

Some things you should let go of
Others you shouldn't
Views differ as to which
I kept hold of everything, just in case"

Just in case I need them for future reference.
Just in case I need to use them against you.
Just in case you use them against me.
Just in case you forget about me.

"I was very young when I was cracked open."

I was told to hold my breath.
I was told to stay calm and lay down.
I was told to duck my head underwater.
I was told to not talk to anyone but you.

"I was very young when I was cracked open."

Just in case you tell someone else.
Just in case you run away from me.
Just in case I need to see a professional.
Just in case I need to remind myself.

"Some things you should let go"
          How do I know what parts?
"Others you shouldn't"
          Why can't I keep it all?
"Views differ as to which"
          Oh, does anyone know?
"I kept hold of everything, just in case"
               Then I guess I shall too.

Emily Berry, The Numbers Game

0003.

"Some days I want to spit me out,
the whole mess of me,
but mostly I am good
and quiet."

I'm not here to be quiet any longer.

Camille Rankine, from Emergency Management